D1055595

# TELEVISION AND OUR CHILDREN

# TELEVISION
## and our
# CHILDREN

By

**ROBERT LEWIS SHAYON**

LONGMANS, GREEN AND CO.
New York · London · Toronto
1951

LONGMANS, GREEN AND CO., INC.
55 FIFTH AVENUE, NEW YORK 3

LONGMANS, GREEN AND CO. Ltd.
6 & 7 CLIFFORD STREET, LONDON W 1

LONGMANS, GREEN AND CO.
215 VICTORIA STREET, TORONTO 1

TELEVISION AND OUR CHILDREN

FIRST EDITION

Printed in the United States of America

To my daughter, Diana,
and the companion legions of her generation:
the challenge
will be theirs, too.

## foreword

THE mid-century year was, among other things, the great year of the television survey. Editors, school principals, and broadcasters vied with one another in measuring television's impact on the rising generation.

No one takes television polls any more—or, at least, not with 1950's attendant blare of trumpets. The agitated waves of public interest have quickly and characteristically subsided. But the problem, for all its familiarity, is still with us.

Here are the children, and there is television, and whether we publicize the grim fact or not, the two new worlds are locked in irrevocable embrace, destined to spin through the years of growing up into tomorrow's questionable maturity.

What are the important facts about these twentieth-century twins? What are the basic insights? Can anything be done to give the relationship a more salutary turn—in the home, and in the community? This book is an attempt to provide some answers.

It is written for parent, teacher, or anyone else who is genuinely concerned about the subject, but who knows little or nothing about the practical considerations of the broadcasting business, and the fundamental concepts of child development that have been formulated in recent years by social scientists.

The book is small, primarily because of original newspaper space limitations: the eight chapters appeared first as a series of articles in *The Christian Science Monitor*, during September, 1950.

Acknowledgement is gratefully made for permission to republish the series in book form. The author is indebted to members of the staff of *The Christian Science Monitor*, who generously assisted in research and editing.

Minor changes have been made in preparing the articles for book publication, in the interests of permanency. No occasion was found, however, to expand their size. As has been observed, of the making of books there is no end these days; and of all the books that are published, there are few that could not say what they have to say more succinctly than they say it.

This book marshals the essentials of its subject and arranges them simply and concisely, without sacrificing required substance.

Although it deals with television, its observations are equally applicable, in general, to the other mass media of communication—the newspapers, magazines, comics, movies, radio, and books.

The information in this volume is a distillation of an area of knowledge that has been familiar to experts in the field for a long time.

Perhaps the chief challenge of our time is not in producing new insights, but rather in more widely communicating old ones that have still to be employed. The author will feel that he will have made a contribution if the book closes somewhat the ubiquitous gap between general reader and expert.

ROBERT LEWIS SHAYON

New York, N. Y.
January, 1951

# introduction

TELEVISION IS NOT like the weather. He who complains about it can do something about it. The trouble is, he usually doesn't.

This is the burden of Mr. Shayon's book, and it is a pointed admonition which should be given the widest possible circulation. In essence, this is a study in responsibility, and it teaches us how responsibility for the character of radio and television programs is shared. Here is no irascible diatribe against commercial sponsors, advertising managers or network executives. Here is no uncritical demand for governmental intervention. Here is, rather, a revealing explanation of the basis upon which the radio-television industry operates, and the limitations within which the Federal Communications Commission must act. This analysis is the prelude to a convincing demonstration that organized group activity and expression of preferences will grease the wheels of progress far more effectively than individual invective.

But this book has another message, perhaps even more important. Commercial television lives by advertising revenues and seeks people in the mass. It will not serve much caviar to the general. It is not its purpose to teach school. Inevitably, commercial television aims to entertain and excite more than educate or enlighten.

These limitations are not the work of individual malefactors but are inherent in the commercial advertising system itself. They can be alleviated by substantial public demand

11

for better or different programs. But is this demand likely to make itself felt in the foreseeable future, particularly if radio and television themselves do little or nothing to stimulate or elevate the public's taste?

There is, in short, only one way to insure that better or different programs will be broadcast and that is to establish radio and television stations that do not depend upon advertising for their financial support. Thus only will the television viewer gain a real range of choice, and thus only can television approach the realization of its great potential value to mankind.

As Mr. Shayon points out, the operation of television stations by educational institutions may help to bring about "television's awakening." In outlining practical prospects for an "awakening" his book should be of great value not only to parents and teachers, but to the public at large.

TELFORD TAYLOR
Counsel to the Joint Committee
on Educational Television

# CONTENTS

**part one**

# THE HOME

CHAPTER

*1*

## the case against TV

*The Mayor was dumb, and the Council stood*
*As if they were changed into blocks of wood,*
*Unable to move a step or cry*
*To the children merrily skipping by,—*
THE PIED PIPER OF HAMELIN

THE PIED PIPER is back. In Hamelin town the wandering fellow wore a gypsy coat of red and yellow. In New York, Fort Worth, Los Angeles, and at all points along the coaxial cable, he comes disguised as a television transmitter. His cunning witchery is piped through air channels estimated to reach 13,000,000 sets by the spring of 1951. And once again, as in old Brunswick land, the Piper hasn't lost his secret charm. The children still come running "merrily after the wonderful music with shouting and laughter." (The Piper, it seems, has always been a mass communicator, whether his messages were aimed at rats, bats, moles, toads, scorpions, or tots.)

Unlike the burghers in Robert Browning's poem, how-

ever, who, by the river Weser, ". . . could only follow
with the eye that joyous crowd at the Piper's back . . . ,"
twentieth-century parents between the Atlantic and the
Pacific are quite vocal in their viewing-with-alarm. Expres-
sions of horror at the allegedly evil effects of television upon
our children, dire prophecies, urgent calls to action, rise in
unremitting chorus from parents, teachers, editorial writers,
government officials, bankers—yes, even advertising executives!

The Cassandra chorus is not the only one heard, however. Television has its disciples, as well as its opponents.
They are as enthusiastic as "the Hamelin people ringing
the bells till they rocked the steeple," when the Piper had
cleared their city of its rats.

Television's admirers don't rock steeples, but they do hail
the new medium as the greatest this, the most wonderful
that, the unlimited everything, according to their particular
interest—salesman, educator, propagandist, artist, and parent
needing the perfect baby sitter.

No one quarrels with great expectations. Indeed, television has already fulfilled many of them with the telecasts
from the United Nations, its coverage of national and local
elections, the communication of such notable cultural events
as the productions of the Metropolitan Opera, and a fair
number of artful and worthwhile entertainment programs.

But we are not concerned with television's virtues. We
propose to examine the grievances that dissenters lay at
TV's expanding screen, report the arguments made in its
defense, and then have a word from the learned experts who
use sound research methods to arrive at useful conclusions.

First, the demurrers. Here is an excerpt from a typical
poll taken by Northwestern University's Professor Paul A.

Witty in Evanston, Illinois. "Parental disapproval [of television] stems from a feeling that programs are too violent, too sensational, too stimulating, and include too many westerns. A surprising number of persons who do not yet own TV sets look upon television with something very close to terror."

The following is a comment from Mrs. Rebecca L. Clark, of Midlothian, Virginia, mother of two children, a son seven and one-half and a daughter five and one-half. (The Clarks had had their television set nearly two years.) "Crime plays like 'The Clock,' 'Lights Out,' etc., are very bad, and I'm surprised that the intelligent men who put on the shows and also the industries that sponsor these programs would show them. They do no one any good and are most harmful to the children who are delinquent in nature or who have no one to guide their thinking. We simply turn off the sets on these programs and so do not hear the advertising product either."

A United Parents Association survey in New York City indicates that the heaviest child viewing of TV is in the age group of five to six years. The tiny ones watch television four hours a day! Effect? Unfavorable. The UPA finds "less interest in active outdoor play, arts and crafts, interference with eating habits, emotional well-being."

Parental concern is not limited to parents outside the broadcasting industry.

*Tide* is the magazine for advertising executives. Advertisers control television. Each month *Tide* canvases a panel of two hundred leaders in advertising, marketing, public relations and kindred fields. On March 31, 1950, the Leadership Panel surveyed "TV & Kids." It reported: "There is strong evidence that panel set owners do not consider tele-

vision an unmixed blessing in the home, at least in respect
to its impact upon children. A heavy majority (67 per cent)
believes that viewing cuts into children's reading and study
time sufficiently to be detrimental to their education. One
states bitterly that he must eat dinner in the dark so the
family can watch TV. Another hails the medium as a great
boon to manufacturers of cowboy suits and toy guns, but
denies it any other virtue."

A letter from a teacher, Mrs. Leland H. Merrill, of
Melrose, Massachusetts, is worth quoting in some length.
"Since 1927 I have maintained a private school for children
of three to six years. About the middle of November (1950),
my assistants began to observe a change. The children 'got'
television.

"Any toy that has any possible resemblance to a gun, becomes one in the free play time; a group barricades itself
in the doll house; another group, armed to the teeth, gallops
up and attacks them. For several days I found drawings, all
done by the same artist, and complementing some conversation which we had heard about 'the Clutching Claw.'

"The children are tired nervously, physically, emotion-
ally, and mentally; they show the effects of eye-strain; they
have acquired erroneous ideas; and their minds are so com-
pletely engrossed by television, that they have no capacity
for learning.

"They have no sense of values, no feeling of wonder, no
sustained interest. Their shallowness of thought and feeling is markedly apparent, and they display a lack of co-
operation and inability to finish a task. Could this be the
result of passively sitting and watching? Or are minds and
bodies alike, too tired?"

Wayne Coy, chairman of the Federal Communications

Commission, the government agency charged with the responsibility of regulating broadcasting in the public interest, spoke at the University of Oklahoma, March 14, 1950. Mr. Coy commented on "the hawkers of horror on radio and television. Our files of letters protesting crime programs are bulging. The situation is rapidly worsening." Mr. Coy also rebuked the networks and warned them about "uninhibited behavior in front of the television camera." Charged Mr. Coy: "Propriety is sacrificed for profits. Clearly there must be a day of reckoning."

Norman Cousins, editor of the *Saturday Review of Literature,* wrote the following widely quoted lines December 24, 1949. "Out of the wizardry of the television tune has come such an assault against the human mind, such a mobilized attack on the imagination, such an invasion against good taste as no other communications medium has known, not excepting the motion picture or radio itself.

"In the one year since television has been on the assembly-line basis, there has been mass-produced a series of plodding stereotypes and low-quality programs. Behind it all, apparently, is a grinding lack of imagination and originality which has resulted in the standardized television formula for an evening's entertainment; a poisoning, a variety show, a wrestling match. . . . All speculation over the future of television must begin with the hard truth that right now it is being murdered in the cradle."

No less imposing an institution than the Royal Bank of Canada feels impelled to comment on the more philosophical problems raised by the new medium. The bank, in its Monthly Letter of July, 1949, remarks: "TV distorts further our picture of the world by diminishing our opportunity to select and isolate the things to which we shall give attention. We grow accustomed to the weirdest of juxtapositions: the serious and the trivial, the comic and the tragic. . . . Here is a collapse of values, a fantasia of effects that resembles the debris left by a storm."

To repeat, this selection of criticism of TV represents only the negative chorus. For every parental dissent there is a parental huzzah. For every teacher shock and gloom—another teacher acclaim. The severest critics often admit TV's good features and point to great possibilities. The same survey shows applause for, as well as condemnation of, identical programs.

In television's behalf, its defenders disagree with its critics about some of its alleged evils, and assert that time will take care of its admitted defects. For every poll indicating that students suffer poorer grades in school because of excessive TV viewing, they present another which shows the opposite.

Samplings, they maintain, are still too isolated and too small to be conclusive. And if excessive viewing should be found to be directly responsible for a drop in marks, improved parental discipline will remedy this, they confidently expect. TV's upset of eating and play habits will also be adjusted in time, they hold.

As for television's effects on children's emotional well-being and taste, this is part of the larger, continuing controversy over the mass media which time does not end, nor the years abate. TV is merely the newest battleground—admittedly the most crucial because it combines the appeals of movies and radio, is easily accessible to the child, and because control of his viewing of it is difficult.

Actually, what effect do mass media have on a child's emotional well-being and taste? After years of patient research, the experts can tell us little that is definitive, one way or another.

Wilbur Schramm, director of the Institute of Communications Research at the University of Illinois, reviewing the effects of mass communications in the *Journalism Quarterly*, December, 1949, sums up a most recent, most authoritative principle this way: "In general, the large amount of escape and entertainment material on the mass media does not change people's interests or behavior patterns, but is rather used in accordance with existing interests and behavior patterns. (That is, persons who have a great deal of social awareness ordinarily select more of that kind of material, less escape material, from the mass media. Persons who have less social awareness select more escape material. Whether the escapist content of the mass media encourages social apathy is not known.)"

It would seem, then, that what television can do to your child will depend on what your child is, what you are educating and guiding him to be, before he looks at television. What part television will play in that shaping is—for the social scientists, and paraphrasing Winston Churchill—a guess wrapped in a conjecture hidden in a speculation.

The alleging, the defending, and the speculating go on. The three choruses counterpoint each other. And the children? What do they think as they follow the Pied Piper, television?

# 2

## the facts about children's televiewing

*For he led us, he said, to a joyous land,*
*Joining the town and just at hand,*
*Where waters gushed and fruit trees grew . . .*
*And everything was strange and new—*
THE PIED PIPER OF HAMELIN

So REPORTED the little boy who was left behind when the Pied Piper of Hamelin lured his playmates through the "wondrous portal opened wide."

A modern child-study expert would suggest that the Brunswick children must have had a deep need for something "strange and new"—otherwise they would not have followed the Piper so blindly through that fateful door in the mountain's side.

What are the important facts about our children's viewing of TV? What is their significance? And what do the children themselves think of the new medium? This chapter will try to answer these questions.

The first important fact is that children see more of all

TV's output—including the programs for grownups—than grownups do.

Cunningham & Walsh, Inc., a New York research organization, has been using "Videotown," a typical American "secret-test" city, as a laboratory on TV since April, 1948. In its third annual census, completed June, 1950, the Cunningham & Walsh survey reports: "The audience viewing TV during an average evening changes, but young children and teen-agers are consistent viewers. Of this young group, 78 per cent are watching television programs on the average night." Note the phrase "average night." This is after the early evening period when children's programs are usually seen.

The "Videotown" report continues: "The least interested TV viewers among Videotown's families are the grown sons and daughters; only 52 per cent of this group are watching television on an average week-day evening. About 30 per cent of the parents in TV families do not watch television programs during the average evening."

The second important fact is the agreement among all observers that children's viewing is "excessive."

The previous chapter noted that the heaviest child viewing of TV is in the age group of five and six years, where the figure is four hours a day. At age five and six, homework is almost nonexistent. From seven years on, viewing tends to diminish, obviously because the school begins to compete for after-hours attention, and also because the growing child begins to develop his own active interests. But three hours a day, which seems to be the average viewing for most children between seven and seventeen, is still, in the opinion of educators and other child-study authorities, "excessive."

Another important fact is that teen-agers seek, in television, to satisfy a hunger for contact with the grownup world, a desire to know, to learn, the urge to participate, a yearning for status.

These needs are easily detected in a survey compiled by Miss Anita Titine Sire, a high-school teacher in New York City. Miss Sire asked two hundred students, ranging in age from fourteen to seventeen, to write about television. Here are some of their replies, with Miss Sire's comments.

"The practical instructions appealed to many. A girl learned to play the ukelele. Sheila learned to dance.

"Travelogues and news were highly praised. They saw celebrities whom they never expected to meet. Stephanie commends the ballet and Paris modes. Sports seemed very popular. Students felt that they were present at the event.

"Eli is astonished. He predicts the end of the theatre. A hand stretches out and gives him a soft drink bottle. He wishes it were so.

"Rita says she doesn't have to read but 'can look and learn.' Eugene finds that a set gives the house an air of distinction.

"Among the programs, the opera was outstanding. Broadway shows were well-liked, the comment being they were unlikely to be seen otherwise."

This fondness of children for opera and Broadway shows on TV also has been observed by Miss Helen Parkhurst, educator, founder of the Dalton School, and creator of the radio program "A Child's World." "Children like shows and opera on TV," agrees Miss Parkhurst, "but what they're really curious about is not the theatre but the grown-up world as seen in the theatre. Our children need contact with that grown-up world, information about it. Actually, our children are among but not with adults. They want to be with, not among."

Returning to Miss Sire's teen-agers, we find that their praise for TV is not unalloyed. Witness the following.

"Some found comedies, mysteries and variety shows stupid, silly, boring, even dangerous. Gloria finds the boxing and wrestling ugly. Stanley's neighbors all walk into the house, sit down, and you have to give them something to eat. When they leave, you have to clean the house.

"Father doesn't mend the fence and mother doesn't do the housework. They lose interest in good books and the theatre. The family is often not in agreement on the choice of programs. This leads to arguments. They eat too fast because a certain program comes on at eight o'clock.

"Aaron doesn't like the advertising but another boy says, 'You see it and you want to buy it.' Miriam cannot knit, sew, or read. There are educational shows but these are the shows that students don't watch.

"Alvin's complaint is, 'When I come home from school each day, I begin to do my work, but suddenly Bob Steele, Tim McCoy, and a posse chase Billy the Kid. When I finish my biology, Howdy Doody has just begun. When I begin my English, Captain Video gives me a shock and in a half hour, I am in Kukla, Fran, and Ollie up to my neck. If I work on my French, Morey Amsterdam hits Newton, the waiter. After having finished my geometry and Spanish, I am dizzy and almost fall down.'"

Apparently, our teen-agers, like their elders, know well the shortcomings of the new medium. And yet—unlike dissenting adults—they watch it avidly. They may be repelled, appalled, offended—but they are fascinated.

Children below the teens seek, in television, to satisfy the same hungers as the adolescents—even to a greater degree, it is suggested, because they are subject to more restrictions than their elder brothers and sisters. This greater amount of restriction seems to develop special needs in this age group for freedom, adventure, excitement.

Florence N. Brumbaugh, director of the Hunter College Elementary School in New York, asked 375 children between the ages of seven and eleven to complete this statement: "If I could choose only one, it would be (books, comics, movies, radios, television) because———." Television won, hands down, of course. Books, surprisingly enough, ran second. Here are some views of seven-to-eleven-year-olds on TV:

"Some of the children said that instead of spending their allowances for the movies, they now used the money for 'snacks' to serve their friends who came in after school for the television programs. 'At the movies,' wrote one boy, 'they make a fuss if you eat popcorn or peanuts, but at home you can have a whole meal while you watch.'"

At home, the figures of the usher, or the movie nurse, stern symbols of the adult, authoritarian world, do not loom above the TV screen.

"Marc sums up his reasons for liking television best in a matter-of-fact fashion. 'It gives you stories like a book, pictures like movies, voices like radio, and adventure like a comic. Television has action while you stay in one spot.'"

To a child, TV is freedom—Marc's own, private four freedoms!

"Nettie, who gives the impression of perpetual motion at school, must settle down now and then at home. Listen to her reasons for liking TV.

"'If I had to choose one, it would be television because many times before I got it, I would say, "Mommy, can't we go to the movies today?" And the answer usually was, "No,

the weather's too bad." Or, "No, I have to go shopping."
But now that we have television, on the rainiest of days,
who wants to go to the movies, when I can watch a cowboy
film? Another thing, at night I have an excuse for staying
up late. "Just let me see the end of this film." "Well, just
this once," says my mother every night. If I didn't have
television, do you think I could find something to do every
night?'"

How can you miss the hint of a vacuum in Nettie's life?

There isn't much representation in the polls for the children under seven. In all likelihood the very little ones would
not be too articulate. Isolated samples of their response run to
this typical form: "I like television because you can see what
is happening"—and to make sure you see the point clearly,
the youthful author of the sentence repeats it with slight
variation, in the best advertising manner, thus: "I like television better than radio because you can see what is happening."

What would the tiny ones say if they knew how? Miss
Brumbaugh puts it as well as any adult can. "The four-
year-old can turn a knob and get a picture that is better than
one in a book because it speaks to him. A six-year-old is not
troubled by hard words that he cannot sound or guess, so
that both find satisfaction in television and can spend long
periods watching the screen."

Knowledge, adventure, excitement, contact with the
grownup world, status, freedom from restriction—these,
then, are all our children's important emotional needs. To
satisfy them they follow the Pied Piper—television. They follow him "excessively."

There can be only two conclusions.

The first is that, apparently, television, like all other mass media, does not really satisfy these hungers of our children. If it did, they would not sit for long periods, passively before screens, in a patient, fruitless vigil of search and unfulfillment. The reason for this is plain: television cannot satisfy these hungers—it is not a genuine experience, but merely a substitute for genuine experience.

The second conclusion is that our children's emotional needs, these days, are "excessive." The reason for this is rather complex but very significant and will be the subject of the next chapter.

# 3

## why children watch TV excessively

*So Willy, let you and me be wipers*
*Of scores out with all men—especially pipers—*
THE PIED PIPER OF HAMELIN

THUS MORALIZES Robert Browning in the last stanza of
"The Pied Piper of Hamelin." If the mayor and the corporation had not reneged on their promise to pay the piper
a thousand guilders, "that strangest figure . . . tall and
thin" would not have stolen away their children.

Great numbers of parents, teachers, and others are afraid
that TV may be trepanning our children into "some sub-
terraneous prison" of mental and emotional evils.

Suggestions for dealing with the problem include, in
characteristic human fashion, such extreme remedies as
pretending the problem doesn't exist, setting up governing
boards, threatening the broadcasters, putting locks on TV
sets, and finally, throwing all sets out of the nearest windows.

According to child-study experts, however, sorely grieved
grownups may not be entirely blameless in this situation.

The experts suggest that, like Hamelin's mayor and corporation, even well-meaning adults may have scores of their own to wipe—with their own children.

This chapter will note these suggestions. It will therefore deal more with adult-child relationships, than with TV, because it is important that we attain an over-all perspective of the problem before we proceed to particular ways of solving it.

In our last chapter we concluded that, generally speaking, our children have "excessive" hungers which they seek, unsuccessfully, to satisfy in TV. These needs are for adventure and excitement, for freedom from restriction, for contact with the grownup world, and for status.

The question is, why are these needs "excessive"? Child psychologists offer one explanation.

They say that children innately possess something that might be called the spirit of liberty. In order to fit them into our civilized society, we train them. Training requires discipline, prohibitions. Improperly applied, these curbs result in frustrations which express themselves in open or secret hostility.

But there seems to be another strong driving force in human behavior, just as powerful as "aggression"—and that is love. Love and affectionate behavior appear in the child's life almost as early as the tendency to aggression does.

If the child's basic needs for love and food are satisfied, if he is respected as an individual with his own tempo of development, the element of aggression can be reduced to what some experts believe to be an irreducible minimum. Other specialists, probably a minority, believe that actual and imaginative aggressive play, wild television programs, comics, even horror movies are harmless ways of releasing this residual aggression. (Child-study experts differ, often sharply, on the degree of harmlessness.)

If a child's basic needs are not satisfied, and the resultant aggression is met with more discipline of the wrong sort, and even parental aggression, a vicious cycle is set in motion which feeds upon itself, creating an "excessive" reservoir of aggression in the child. Such a child, whether he rebels openly or becomes deceptively obedient, develops a craving for violence and fantasy which drives him continually to the mass media, particularly TV. There the child finds unlimited fare but no wholesome satisfaction for an abnormal appetite.

That, in brief, is the explanation offered by the child psychologists. A second explanation is advanced by the social scientists, and it is ably expounded by Mrs. Dorothy Lee, a cultural anthropologist at Vassar College, and a consultant for the Midcentury White House Conference on Children and Youth, held in Washington, December, 1950.

Our children, declares Mrs. Lee, "are our great minority group; we exclude them from all effective sharing in the life of the family or the community. We cheat them of their right to be effectively creative, to have a responsible and significant role in society. The ideal we set up for all Americans, in our schools, our writings, and our lectures, is one where a child's activities are carefully sterilized so that they have no effect on our closed adult world."

"Of course," adds Mrs. Lee, "we do it for their sake; we relieve them of the 'burden' of responsibility; we give them freedom to play instead of to work. And because we feel that something is lacking, we are spurred to do more and more for them, to make greater sacrifices, to inconvenience ourselves a little further. For their sake, we leave our cherished apartment to live in a house, or we move from the city to a dull suburb. We mess up our free Saturday to take them to a museum, or wear ourselves out walking around the zoo with them. Yet in all this, we speak of 'our' and 'their.' We are the adults; the family, the community, the school, they are the outsiders."

Mrs. Lee is no mere pedagogue in this matter of raising children. She has four of her own. She continues:

"We do not give our children the chance to make a dent in our lives. We change our plans for them, but do we change them with them? We buy the cereals they make us buy because of the Superman mask or the model of the ghost town; but do we ever let them plan the day's menu and actually base our meal on their suggestions? We spend much time and care teaching skills to our children. We teach them how to do things, not to do things."

There, briefly, we have the cultural explanation to the question: Why are the needs which our children seek to satisfy in TV "excessive"?

No clear line divides these two explanations. Exclusion, as well as discipline, may cause aggression. A child, locked out of his parents' world, may feel hostile and seek to punish them by too much televiewing. Discipline itself is a form of exclusion. And so on. Taken together, the two theories may not provide the whole answer, but the social scientists, at this time, feel that they would be the most important part of any valid answer.

If the experts are correct, then we grownups are definitely not without blame in this difficulty with our Pied Piper, television. Apparently, we give our children too much of the wrong kind of discipline, not enough respect for their development as individuals, and we exclude them from our adult world.

We may commit these faults out of a mistaken sense of love, out of laziness, neglect, ignorance, or simply because our own lives are too busy to permit us to do otherwise. Nevertheless, the faults are committed. Is it any wonder, ask the specialists, that many of our children have turned, in desperation, to the mass media, and are now turning to the newest, most fascinating, most potent medium—television?

Television has no sign on it: "Trespassers will be prosecuted." Television is living made easy for our children. It is the shortest cut yet devised, the most accessible back door to the grownup world. Television is never too busy to talk to our children. It never shunts them off because it has to prepare dinner. Television plays with them, shares its work with them. Television wants their attention, needs it, goes to any lengths to get it.

Television brings them people to meet; it informs them, gives them things to do—win prizes, send in box tops. Television says to each child, four, fourteen, and often beyond into the restricted lives of many immature grownups: "You are the center of my universe—my Aladdin. I am your genie. Command your wildest dream—and you shall have it—instantly—at the touch of your fingers!"

The child wants to be "in" on the exciting world of adult life. We put him into cocoons, set him apart in schools. We delay, as long as possible, his full membership in adulthood's private club. In the early life of this nation, in its frontier phase, a child, from the time he could crawl and gather sticks for the fire, became a contributing member of the family and community. He went to work at an early age, learned a trade, married young.

Today our children must wait to earn a living, wait to marry and establish homes of their own. Only in one respect they do not wait—and that is, to grow. To grow means to want and need genuine experiences, not contrived, manufactured substitutes.

No, the Pied Piper is not the only villain in the piece. However, this does not mean that those who are influencing the development of TV are absolved of all responsibility. The home is not the sole source of the difficulty. Rather is this a problem for all adults—parents, teachers, broadcasters, government officials, advertisers—whatever their interests.

For all other interests are as nothing if they are not directed to the furthering of our only true interest—the making of our children into mature, responsible citizens, capable of preserving the best in our democratic heritage and forwarding it.

The Midcentury White House Conference on Children and Youth provided useful road signs along the way. Previous conferences dealt primarily with children's more material needs—physical, social, economic. The theme of the 1950 conference was "For every child—a fair chance for a healthy personality." And by "personality" the conference did not mean charm or temperament. It meant the sum total of the mental, emotional, and spiritual qualities essential to individual happiness and responsible citizenship.

Conference workers were unanimous in their feeling that the need for such an orientation is pressing. "Why," asked Ruth Kotinsky, assistant director of fact finding for the conference—"why, at this midcentury mark, a shift in emphasis, a turn to concern with the happiness of all the children? Is it merely that enough information is already at hand about more tangible services? Or is it rather because too large a proportion of those children for whom adequate services are available still fail to achieve wholesome maturity? Is the dark shadow of the times making itself felt?"

All adults must begin to realize that the dark side of television is but another symptom of a deep-lying trouble in our time. It is not television that must be cured. It is not even our children. It is we, the grownups—you, I, our neighbor. It is all of us and the values by which we live.

To understand this is to grasp the tail of the television serpent, preparatory to turning it into a rod of power—for good.

# 4

## winning the home-front war against the pied piper

*The Mayor sent East, West, North, and South,*
*To offer the Piper by word of mouth,*
*Silver and gold to his heart's content,*
*If he'd only return the way he went,—*
THE PIED PIPER OF HAMELIN

ACCORDING TO Browning, that is how the parents of Hamelin tried to recover their lost children after the Pied Piper had lured the town's spellbound youngsters through a door in a mountain's side.

Modern parents are more fortunate than the burghers of Brunswick. Our children are under the spell of the new Pied Piper—television—but they are still, figuratively speaking, this side of the mountain. There is still time to act.

Many parents are acting—in their homes. They have declared open war on the Piper and they are using an assortment of weapons to prosecute it.

What are these weapons? In the opinion of child-study

experts, are they desirable? Are well-intentioned fathers and mothers, unknowingly, taking ineffective measures? Worse—are they doing things that are actually harmful?

In this chapter, we will consider and evaluate the war against the Pied Piper on the home front.

The simplest weapon being used, of course, is the direct boycott of TV. As a mother in Chicago put it, in a letter to a newspaper editor: "This is one family's solution to the TV problem. The most important thing is not to have a set."

How widely this weapon is being wielded it is impossible to say. Certainly, the boycott is not very prevalent among lower-income parents who have not enjoyed the fullest educational advantages. The surveys indicate that such parents regard TV as an unalloyed blessing. TV provides continuous, low-cost entertainment in their homes, and it keeps their children occupied and, supposedly, "out of trouble."

The boycott is, probably, most popularly enlisted by middle-class parents with good educational backgrounds. These parents usually take a calm, well-reasoned, and persuasive attitude in explaining their stand. The following expression from a mother in California is typical of their arguments.

"We do not have a television set. We do not have any particular desire to have one since we use the radio itself so little. I can teach B——— (a three-year-old daughter) and entertain her in the happy, positive way of life with books and guided indoor and outdoor living. Radio and television are more hazard than help to my own mental growth. I feel the same will be true when B——— is old enough to listen."

It is perfectly possible, of course, to have normal, happy children in a TV-less home. However, child-study experts point out that there are weaknesses to this cutting-of-the-Gordian-knot method. The most obvious weakness is that no child today, even in rural areas, can really be isolated from television. TV grows more omnipresent with each passing hour. If your child does not watch it at home, he will, sooner or later, see it at your neighbor's, even at school, or elsewhere.

To be "out" in this respect is, even for the most balanced child, to suffer severe stresses which he may be reluctant to disclose to his parents. No matter how lovingly, and with what taking-into-confidence, according to your child's capacity to understand, you exclude him from the actual world about him, you are taking advantage of the heavy hand of your parental authority. It is far better, say the experts, to take the TV dragon into your house, where, at least, you can have a fair go at him.

"Regulation" seems to be the heavy artillery in the battle against the Piper. It is, by far, the method most favored by all who are expressing themselves on the child-TV problem. Teachers urge you to regulate your child's televiewing. So do other parents who are "successfully" regulating. Even broadcasters, who are, to say the least, extremely sensitive to the word "regulation" when it is applied to their industry practises, are enthusiastically for home regulation of children's TV habits.

On the face of it, regulation appears to be logical. Your child does not know what to watch or when, or how long to view. You, the parent, know. You must tell your child, and he must obey. It is all so simple—and, of course, it relieves every one but you of any responsibility.

As in the case of the direct boycott, well-meaning, well-educated parents apply the theory of regulation in an atmosphere of assuredly benevolent paternalism. Here is how one mother describes her use of regulation.

"I have two girls, five and seven. Naturally, they have been interested in television, but I think we have kept the upper hand so far. They see only the children's programs, and never more than an hour at a time; usually half an hour or less. We have drawn the line at westerns so far."

Another mother of two children states: "We have a rule that, regardless of what is on television, bedtime is at eight. I have kept this rule lovingly, but firmly, and my children go off to bed without a single argument."

Many experts say that "keeping the upper hand," "drawing the line," "having a rule regardless"—no matter how "lovingly and firmly" done—smacks of dictatorship, not democracy, in the home, and may not always be wise. Of course, a child may go to bed without a single argument because it has participated in a decision to do so, and willingly accepts it, but, generally speaking, flat fiats handed down from above, in homes as in governments, make for openly rebellious or overly docile individuals.

This is not to make an unqualified case for a technique of raising children, in which they are allowed to do as they please. Each parent, naturally, must find his own balance between freedom and discipline, a balance which can be democratically administered. The strong tower of regulation is a child's real understanding for the necessity of it. The quicksand of regulation, as with the boycott, is that the child cannot always be directly under a parent's control —or even gentle guidance. Outside the home, he is bound to meet powerful temptations to depart from the "regulations" that a parent has imposed, and the price he must pay for struggling to resist them may be too high in terms of emotional well-being.

Apparently, the twin weapons of bribery and punishment are still used by many well-meaning parents. Affirms one mother: "The first year [of having a TV set] the children washed supper dishes before TV programs. When their attitude toward dishes was poor—no TV for a week." Another mother declares: "We use TV in disciplining the children too. That is, if they misbehave at the dinner table, for instance, no TV!"

The child-study specialists universally frown on these modern versions of old "candy for a good child" and "supperless to bed for a naughty child" methods of discipline. Wise discipline, they suggest, aims not at strengthening the parent's authority, but rather at strengthening the child's self-control and sense of responsibility. In well-ordered homes, the experts maintain, such bribes and punishments are entirely unnecessary.

"Family viewing of TV" is commonly practiced with a widely held belief that it is a potent cure-all for the ills of TV. The experts approve of family viewing, but with an important qualification. Charles A. Siepmann, a leading authority on mass media, states the qualification this way, in his book *Radio, Television, and Society*: "There are those who question whether a family grouped in silence around a television receiver is in any true sense favorably affected in terms of family relationships.

"The development of common interests within a family is obviously desirable, and common experience is an essential basis of personal relations. But much depends upon the nature of the experience and its life-giving quality. Maybe it will take more than television to make a home into a family."

Watching TV with the children is mentioned as a salutary factor in all reports from parents who seem to be having little or no trouble with TV. But corollary to it are selective rather than promiscuous viewing, discussing programs critically and constructively with the children, evaluating them, using the programs as springboards from which to launch higher the child's information about the world and his understanding of its values. If the child learns standards, not in any formal atmosphere of instruction, but rather in the informal, democratic experience of his family, he will tend to use these standards when he is away from the family group.

The following excerpts from letters to a newspaper would be applauded by child-study experts.

Mrs. Clinton Smart, of Pasadena, California, writes: "We never turn on TV and take it as it comes continually. We know what programs the children see, because we watch TV with them. We often get out the globe to see where some place is in relation to our own."

Mrs. Maude V. Eaton, of Washington, D. C.: "When we know what the children are seeing and hearing, we find it possible to bring out ideas and ask and answer questions."

A letter signed by Mr. and Mrs. P. M. Knox, Jr., of Baltimore, states: "Children love to be happy. It is inherent in their being. Therefore, the strongest appeal I have found for being selective in their programs is to make them aware of the results—whether or not any feeling of joy or real satisfaction was theirs as a result of listening to a certain program. Using this for a measuring rod, we all soon became aware that any program which takes away our sense of happiness, isn't worth it. Most of the time the children seem to have no desire to see the morbid, uninspirational type of thing."

In many cases, these desirable methods of meeting television's threat are combined with undesirable ones. Parents who selectively and critically view TV with their children often exhibit autocratic tendencies in the matter of regulation and discipline. The principle of selection might be usefully applied to methods of guidance as well as to programs selected in efforts to solve the problem of child-TV viewing.

Most important of all, the problem should not be viewed as a special one, but as part of the larger problem of the child's growth in terms of his individuality. This philosophy of growth is heavily underscored by the child-study experts. We must not try to mold our children as though they were so much clay, they tell us. Clay does not grow. Nor are our children bundles of conditioned reflexes. They are individuals, subject to laws of development.

We may assist the child in his development, but he must do his own growing. We must not pay too much attention to mere training and instruction. Our central task as parents is to discover and to respect individuality, even in the child of tender age. There must be more tolerance, more kindness, and much more fun and humor in homes.

The story of Sam Bryan in New York City is an indication that the TV "problem" need not necessarily be a problem at all.

Sam Bryan is eleven years old. He has known TV in his home ever since he was two. It is part of the natural world he is growing up in.

"Do you like TV better than books?" we asked Sam.

"It depends on the program and the book," was his answer. "If there's really a terrific program, like a World Series game, I'd rather see it. I can read a book later. If the program isn't exciting, I'll take the book." The same applies to playing baseball or watching it on TV. Sam does not read

more or less since the number of TV programs has increased
—just about the same.

He is not too interested in crime or murder programs. He
has seen only four in the last two or three years. His interest
in sports has increased. He learns baseball from the best
professional players. In entertainment—singing, dancing,
etc.—his standards have been raised because he sees the best.
He has not withdrawn from activity and become just a spec-
tator. He still plays catch every day and baseball twice a
week.

It would seem that Sam Bryan has TV and not TV Sam
Bryan. He knows how to appraise TV, select from it what
is useful and wholesome, and reject the rest. TV is merely
another tool he uses to build a full life. That is a sound
relationship between a boy and a television set.

TV is a group experience for the Bryans. They view together, they talk about the programs afterward. We would
guess that there are no heavy rules or regulations in the
Bryan household, that their family life is neither adult-
oriented or child-oriented—simply family-oriented.

Even television as it is now, with all its faults, can be
used fruitfully by discerning parents. The recipe is simple.
Take a good look at your homes to see whether they are
democracies or dictatorships, benevolent or otherwise. Don't
shut your children out—let them share your responsibilities.
They can ask for no greater privilege. Respect them as individuals. Watch TV with them critically, constructively.

The Pied Piper will soon surrender. He cannot win
against such weapons.

# part two
# THE COMMUNITY

# 5

## why the broadcasters act as they do

*When suddenly, up the face*
*Of the Piper perked in the market-place,*
*With a, "First, if you please, my thousand guilders!"*
THE PIED PIPER OF HAMELIN

THE PIED PIPER, you may recall, was, professionally, a socially useful individual. He wandered about Asia and Europe, practicing his charm chiefly "on creatures that do people harm. . . ." Naturally, he charged a fee for his services. Even pipers, apparently, must eat and pay rent. It was only when he had rid Hamelin of its rats, and the mayor and corporation had tried to cheat him of 950 guilders, that the piper, in a pique, absconded with the town's youngsters.

In the United States, the men who manage television— today's Pied Piper—are certainly not motivated by desire to cast a spell over our children. Most of them surely are fathers themselves. Like the Piper, they are also businessmen. They render services and expect—even as you and I—to be paid accordingly.

What do the citizen-fathers who operate television think of the effects their new medium is having on children?

This chapter considers the economic nature of TV, and examines what light the business consideration has to throw upon the problem of our children and television.

Like all Gaul, TV in the United States is divided into three chief parts—the sponsor, the advertising agent, and the station owner.

The sponsor pays the station owner for his time and other facilities. The advertising agent acts as middleman between the sponsor and the station owner, for which the sponsor pays him a commission. The man who pays, you will observe, is the sponsor; and you and I, the public, pay the sponsor by buying his goods or services. The important relationship, then, is the one between the sponsor and the public.

If you were to ask a hypothetical sponsor why he puts on certain presumably "harmful" television programs, he might, first, brusquely ask by whose authority the programs are judged "harmful." You would, then, have to admit that the social sciences have no empirical data to support such an accusation. The best you could do would be to point out that many experts, after much scholarly observation, have charged that many TV programs are harmful. But you would have to admit that, from an objective standpoint, the experts so far have proved nothing.

Not content to abandon your inquiry, however, you might continue addressing our imaginary sponsor thus: "In human affairs, we guide our actions by many forces which are not capable of being pragmatically tested. You cannot entirely brush aside the considered judgment of many highly trained, informed, and sensitive observers."

If the sponsor were candid he might drop his challenging attitude and take you, with confidence, into the heart of his dilemma. He would point out that TV, like the newspapers, the magazines, or the radio, is simply another medium which he uses to advertise his products; and that, in accord with prevailing custom and practice in business, he cannot justify spending a dollar in advertising unless it will bring more dollars in sales.

Continuing his confidential explanation, our sponsor would probably go on to say that he, personally, would like nothing better than to be able to put on television programs which everyone would find wholesome and unobjectionable. But his prime goal is, still, to maintain and increase sales. In order to do this, at justifiable cost, via TV, he must attract large audiences.

His advertising agent, who specializes in such matters, tells him that the only way to attract large audiences is to put on programs that attract the public. The programs that attract the public, according to the advertising agent, are, more often than not, the very ones which the critics consider either positively harmful, or, at the very least, negatively unsatisfactory.

How, asks the sponsor, is he to escape from his dilemma?

To put on most so-called "good" programs is to risk public inattention, and loss of sales. To lose sales is to suffer the disapproval of, and possible penalties from, his corporation and its stockholders. On the other hand, with no scientific evidence that the "bad" programs are really detrimental; with the public, so his advertising agent tells him, pleased with them; and with his sales curves, as a result, showing marked—in some cases remarkable—rises, what choice has he but to continue as he is doing at present?

At this point, our hypothetical sponsor might, conceivably, remind you that he is a father himself; he might even admit that he occasionally has secret misgivings about the whole matter. But it would be a brave executive indeed, he would argue, who, sitting in a little, minority rowboat, would dare pull against the strong tide of the "practical" situation.

In conclusion, if he were shrewd, the sponsor would simply and fairly ask what you would do, if you were in his place.

Wisely withholding your answer, your next step would be to have an equally frank talk with the sponsor's advertising agent. "On what basis," you might ask him, "do you advise your client that the programs which critics consider 'unsatisfactory' and 'harmful' are the very ones that attract the public?"

The advertising agent would reply that his recommendations are based on the vast amount of data accumulated by all known methods that measure the preference of audiences. These methods include telephone calls to, and personal interviews with, TV listeners, automatic devices that record the stations to which a set is tuned, and the keeping of listener diaries.

The agent would admit that all these methods have their limitations, but he would insist that they have always indicated that the majority of listeners generally prefer the kind of programs which are being put on, rather than the kind that TV critics are always badgering the sponsor to produce. By and large, the advertising agent would assert, the figures prove that the people like what they are getting on TV.

If you were armed with the counterarguments that the critics are accustomed to employ in such a debate (and it has been going on for some time), you would then ask the agent how people can be expected to like what they do not get. You would declare that the record shows that the so-called "desirable" programs are, with certain rare exceptions, never put on at times when the largest audiences are available to see them, that is, during the early evening hours; and that when a "good" program is put on at a favorable period, it is hardly ever there long enough to give the listeners an opportunity to grow to like it.

Here, the advertising agent might do two things. He might call you a tiresome, professional "intellectual," say that he has heard all your stale arguments before, and show you to the door. Or perhaps, impressed by your genuine desire to understand, he might, as did the sponsor before him, take you into his confidence.

In the latter case, he would admit, "off the record," that there is some merit to your arguments. If he is a father, he might disclose that, sometimes, on his commuter's special, in one of those rare moments when he is not concentrating on how to hold that shaky account, he worries about the situation. But what, he would ask, is the alternative?

Deliberately to advise a client that he experiment with an untried program formula, and thus fly in the face of every trade shibboleth, would be to risk a fearsome drop in the sponsor's sales curve.

The advertising business is highly competitive, the agent would declare, and clients are known to be notoriously fickle, sometimes changing agencies with the proverbial speed of the pea in the shell game. Where, the agent would ask, is the man so free, so clear of all encumbering professional and private pressures and obligations, that he may, like Don Quixote, go recklessly tilting at audience windmills?

"No," the advertising agent would conclude, "this is a situation in which my hands are tied. The facts may be regrettable, but what can I do?" And just before you took your leave, he might, profitably, repeat the sponsor's disturbing query: "What would you do if you were in my place?"

More reluctant to answer, you might then go to the station owner who carries the programs the advertising agent recommends to the sponsor.

"I have been told," you might say, "that TV station owners are licensed by the government to operate in the public interest. I can understand, perhaps, how circumstances tend to compel the sponsor and the advertising agent to perpetuate the unsatisfactory program situation.

"But I do not understand why you, the station owner, vested as you are with the responsibility of protecting the public's interest, do not take immediate steps to remedy the situation."

The station owner, intuitively sensing that, by now, you would be impatient with all the customary platitudes, evasions, and rationalizations about "giving the people what they want" and practicing "cultural democracy," would quickly come to the root of the matter.

He would tell you that late in 1945, and again in 1947, the National Association of Broadcasters financed a nationwide investigation of the public's attitude toward radio. When the investigation was completed, the N.A.B. hired Dr. Paul F. Lazarsfeld, the head of Columbia University's Bureau of Applied Social Research, to analyze the findings.

Since radio's pattern is, obviously, being extended to

television, the station owner would suggest that there is no reason why Dr. Lazarsfeld's conclusions cannot be applied with equal validity to TV. He would then read you what Dr. Lazarsfeld said, after reviewing the conventional arguments for and against "serious" and "educational" broadcasting.

"Few people want to learn by way of radio, but most critics agree that they should. Therefore the best thing for the broadcaster to do is to keep the volume of educational broadcasts slightly above what the masses want. In this way, he may contribute to a systematic rise in the general cultural level without defeating the educational goal by driving the audience away. This policy will disappoint some educators, and bore some listeners, but it is precisely the kind of compromise which must be found."

That is Dr. Lazarsfeld's conclusion. After reading it to you, our hypothetical station owner might, if he were quite candid, state flatly that the proposed Lazarsfeld compromise is simply out of the question. A station's chief revenue, he would remind you, comes from the sponsor. It is the sponsor who decides what is put on.

The station owner might, obligingly, tell you that there are proposals on record for solving the problem. These include the production of programs by the station itself, and the limiting of the sponsor to the advertising message; the dictating to the sponsor of what kind of programs he may produce; and the arbitrary setting aside of specific periods of time for station-produced programs with no advertising at all.

All these solutions, the station owner would assert, are unworkable. Unless an owner were eager to commit financial suicide, he could not possibly attempt to effect any such measures singlehanded. Universal agreement by all station owners to do the same would be necessary. It is a matter of record that station owners have never been able to agree on anything more meaningful than a harmless decency code.

Besides, each of the proposed solutions would mean either direct expense to the station owner or loss of revenue from the sponsor. The average station owner can afford neither of these choices, particularly at this crucial moment in TV's development, when all his assets are being plowed back into a fierce, competitive struggle for a place in television's future. The future is expected to be highly profitable but, at present, is enormously expensive.

When the station owner had finished, you might ask if he could suggest any way at all out of the dilemma. "Yes," he might say, "let the public make its wishes known to the sponsors." But if you protested that letter-writing campaigns and organized pressure groups face too many obvious obstacles, and that, consequently, they have failed, in the past, to have any significant results, our station owner would probably shake his head, and reply: "I cannot deny it. But that is democracy. The machinery is there, but the people do not use it as fully as they should. As a father and a citizen, I am concerned. But I am a businessman; what would you do if you were in my place?"

By now, having traversed all of television's Gaul, you are ready, like Caesar, to make your own commentary.

The sponsor, the advertising agent, and the station owner have compelling reasons for putting on the kind of television programs that we see and hear. In order to challenge the pattern, they would have to accept serious financial risk. The more thoughtful among TV executives know full well that the social consequences of their actions may not be wholly desirable—even for their own children. Yet they continue to perpetuate the unhappy cycle of cause and effect.

This ethical duality, of course, is not unique to the television business. It cuts across the whole range of our way of life. It is that old problem of our double standard of socio-economic morality.

You should be prepared, now, to answer the thrice-repeated question: "What would you do if you were in my place?"

Your right to sit in judgment on the men of television depends on the integrity of your reply.

# 6

## the F.C.C. looks to you

Do you know that you, if you live in the United States, own television's airwaves?

This question may startle you. Yet, in 1947, a national poll of the public's attitude toward broadcasting disclosed that only 50 per cent of a representative cross-section of listeners were aware that government, representing you, has anything to do with the operation of radio (and TV) stations; 16 per cent actually denied it; 34 per cent did not know.

The Federal Communications Commission in Washington is the seven-member government agency which, on your behalf, issues licenses to individual broadcasters to operate TV stations in your interest.

What does the F.C.C., your agency, have to report to you about television's unsatisfactory impact upon children? What are your seven commissioners doing to help solve this problem? Do they have specific recommendations to make —and to whom?

This chapter considers the role of the Federal Communications Commission in the child-TV situation; and, as in our first five chapters, it brings the matter back to the same doorstep—the one marked "citizen-parents," regardless of their special interests.

Are the members of the F.C.C. concerned about TV's negative effects on children? At least two commissioners have declared publicly that they are. Wayne Coy, chairman of the commission, addressed the Annual Radio Conference on Station Problems at the University of Oklahoma, March 14, 1950.

"The American home," Mr. Coy said, "is not a night club. It is not a theatre. It is not a midway. The attitude that people bring to those places is not the attitude they bring to their homes or suffer others to bring." He referred to the "risqué, ribald, raffish sort of thing we are getting," and said, "I think it is far better for the radio station licensees and the networks to clean house before public opinion demands the more drastic remedy of governmental action."

Mr. Coy also said: "Our [the commission's] files of letters protesting crime programs are bulging. The situation is rapidly worsening."

Looking ahead into TV's future, Mr. Coy prophesied: "I see some indications of a trend to inferior programming . . . because of the expense . . . and because of the desire of television broadcasters and television network operators to reduce their losses or to get larger profits."

With respect to the crime programs, however, the chairman of the F.C.C. did not mention any possible governmental action. The explanation may be found in the fact that the Federal Communications Act of 1934, under which the F.C.C. operates, specifically declares obscenity and profanity to be a violation of the law, whereas there is nothing in the act to indicate that crime programs, however horrorful they may be, are illegal.

Miss Frieda B. Hennock is the other member of the F.C.C. who has expressed herself publicly on the quality of TV's programs. Miss Hennock is the newest commissioner and the only woman member of the F.C.C. The following are excerpts from a speech she made at the Institute for Education by Radio, Columbus, Ohio, May 4, 1950:

"As long as the objectives of American broadcasting are commercial it isn't going to go very far to make radio a creative force in our society. . . . Your primary concern and mine is programming, and it is far from satisfactory. Instead of programs which are designed to develop an enlightened public opinion or to aid in the cultural development of our people, we get for the most part programs molded in the fire of business competition, and whose salutary effects are merely incidental.

"Horror and crime programs for children, soap operas for adults—there is no need to go through the whole list. I am sure you know what I am referring to and I am also sure that the first question that occurs to many of you is why doesn't the F.C.C. do something about it."

Thus speak two members of the Federal Communications Commission, your government agency, charged by Congress with regulating the broadcasting industry in your interest.

What is the answer to Miss Hennock's self-directed question? It is a threefold one. First, you the people have not told your commission clearly what you want it to do; second, you have not given it the money required to do the job; and third, even if your instructions were clear, even if you did provide the money with which to carry them out, the F.C.C., as presently constituted, would be reluctant, arbitrarily, to impose your will on the broadcasters.

We will examine the three parts of the answer separately.

First: the matter of your instructions to the F.C.C.

As noted above, this agency operates under the Communications Act passed by Congress in 1934. Basically, Congress granted to the commission the power to issue and revoke station licenses, and to police the technical aspects of airwave traffic. In addition to banning obscene language, and profanity, as pointed out above, it also prohibited lotteries. It asked that rival candidates for political offices be given equal time on the air.

However, except for these specific provisions relating to the content of programs rather than to their technical flow, Congress said nothing about the commission's duty to regulate the nature of the programs that broadcasters may put on. Indeed, in one section of the law, Congress definitely withheld from the commission the power of censorship and the right to interfere with free speech. Congress gave the F.C.C. only one general principle by which to guide its actions in the field of program material. This is the rather ambiguous instruction to see that all broadcasting conformed "to the public interest, convenience, or necessity."

"Now, if you were a member of the Federal Communications Commission, and you were concerned about "bad" TV programs, how would you interpret your powers, under the law, with respect to doing something constructive about those programs? Would you maintain, as some commissioners in the past have done, that the F.C.C. may have the duty and power to tell a station owner licensee what kind of programs he should put on, as well as the right to revoke his license if he refuses to comply with the commission's requests?

And by what measuring rod would you arrive at what constituted a desirable, fair, and balanced program pattern? Is that censorship?

Even to state the problem simply is to suggest its enormous complexity.

Or would you say, as other commissioners have, that what Congress clearly intended, in writing the law, was that this responsibility for the kind and the quality of the programs we see on television should be left to the stations themselves, in touch with the special needs of their respective communities?

The dilemma has plagued the industry since its inception. Controversy concerning it continues unabated, to this moment. Many experts who have given the matter a great deal of serious thought have suggested that the United States Supreme Court could resolve the issue if a test case were brought before it. The court could rule on the constitutionality of the debated provisions of the Communications Act.

To date, however, the F.C.C. has not initiated any test case before the Supreme Court, probably because the question of constitutionality is not the ultimate one. The final question is whether any proposed course of action arising out of any interpretation of the law is workable, equitable, and wise. In the last analysis, this problem can be solved only by Congress.

Your representatives in Congress have taken no recent steps to solve the problem. Why? No doubt because, in the last several years, your harried senators and representatives have been subject to more pressing demands on their time and energies.

Another explanation may be that the issue of government regulation of broadcasting is loaded with political dynamite. It goes to the very heart of the great and delicate questions of our era—the questions often labeled "socialism vs. free enterprise," and "regimentation vs. the freedom of the individual in our society."

The broadcasting industry, like other important institutions in this country, maintains an active lobby on Capitol Hill. Charles A. Siepmann, in his book *Radio, Television, and Society*, states: " . . . the radio industry for the most part resents the fact that the government has been allotted an important contributory role in the operation of the system; it would prefer to be entirely free from any subordination to the government. Indeed, its current ambition is to achieve freedom identical with that of press and films."

Your representatives in Congress might fairly ask you: "Do you know your own mind on these momentous questions? Are you adequately informed and fully aware of the possible consequences of suggested proposals? Are you communicating to us what you wish to do about these problems?"

The fact that probably half of the citizens of our nation do not even know of the existence of the Federal Communications Commission is cause for sober reflection.

Examining the second of Miss Hennock's questions—is there money for the job?—let us suppose that Congress did grant clear and unmistakable powers to the F.C.C. to judge television's program content. It would also have to grant, along with those powers, sufficient funds for a staff large enough to carry out the tremendous task of merely keeping the records of what goes out over the air, let alone the job of evaluating the information gathered.

Congress has never been generous in granting funds to the F.C.C. The commission's staff is small, its budget meager—considering its heavy work load of regulating all radio, wire, and cable services. In 1949, the total staff numbered 1,327 persons; the appropriation by Congress was only a little more than $6,000,000.

By far the larger part of the commission's staff is technical. The other large department is legal.

There is no department of program research.

Third: the wisdom of program control of censorship.

Mr. Coy, the F.C.C. chairman, in his Oklahoma address, said: "I must make it clear that I do not think the commission . . . now has the competence or will ever have the competence to determine the kinds of programs that we should see and hear. . . . More than that, I think it would be highly dangerous for seven people to have such authority. The real control of American radio is in the hands of the public. . . ."

Miss Hennock, in her Ohio speech quoted above, declared: "Even with such a [larger] staff we could not raise the standard of American broadcasting to what it should be. You can accuse us of being soft or of being lenient, but believe me, by withholding a few licenses we could not ensure better programming. You are looking to the wrong place. . . . The affirmative job must rest ultimately on the broadcaster and the public. . . .

"I have learned that there is no quick cure for what ails American broadcasting and I have learned that the F.C.C. is not the physician.

"It's you."

Evidently, then, there is not much point in looking to your Federal Communications Commission to reduce the larger negative factors in TV programming, or directly to enforce any positive factors. At best, by its own present definition, the F.C.C. can only perform a rear-guard action in American broadcasting. For a frontal attack on the problem, your F.C.C. is looking to you.

What does your commission want you to do?

Mr. Coy urges you to overcome apathy and organize into local, state and national listener councils all over America. A nucleus of such groups is already functioning in the country. Mr. Coy would like to see them grow—in number and in size. Mr. Coy believes that "such organizations could be of great assistance not only to the industry and to the Federal Communications Commission, but to the Congress which writes our radio laws.

"I would like to see these listener groups represented at hearings in their communities involving applications for new stations, or for renewals of license of present stations, or for transfer of control of existing stations. I would like to see them well represented in hearings before the commission in Washington and in every discussion involving changes in our broadcasting policies. . . . The time has come for the listener to make himself heard—not in sporadic, exasperated outbursts, but in an intelligent, rational, organized fashion. In union there is strength. The listener council movement can become one of the most powerful agencies for the public good in our time."

Miss Hennock is convinced "that the healthiest thing for American broadcasting would be for education and educators to be right in the thick of it. . . . We have got to get some people into broadcasting who are interested in benefiting the public and we have to get the public interested in benefiting itself. A good portion of American programming must be designed to help the public, not merely to perpetuate its limitations.

"We need programs which will emphasize our great cultural heritage; we need programs which will effectively prepare and assist our people to assume the responsibilities of citizenship in a great democracy. The way to do it is to have noncommercial interests an integral part of radio and television. And it is on educators that I lay the principal burden for doing this."

The assumptions of Mr. Coy and Miss Hennock are valid. No doubt, if there is to be any positive, constructive action taken to improve present TV program standards, it can only, realistically, come from the two indicated directions. But are there difficulties inherent in action by listeners and educators? What does past experience teach us about their chances for success? Can the challenges of Mr. Coy and Miss Hennock be met effectively?

We will consider these questions in our final chapters.

# 7

## the listener council movement

GEORGE BERNARD SHAW said, "Get what you want or you will be forced to like what you get." The Irish playwright's aphorism has special vigor when it is applied to what parents would like television to offer their children—at least in the United States.

Can parents get what they want in this respect? What are the ways and means by which citizen viewers can exercise their democratic right to bring about an improvement in TV fare?

Many listener viewers, of course, seem entirely satisfied with what they are getting. Others have adopted a grin-and-bear-it attitude: they "don't particularly mind" or they are willing to "put up" with TV programs as they are. Perhaps the satisfied and the tolerant might think otherwise if they knew that TV could provide, if not "better," then, at least, different programs.

The fact that a probable majority of TV set owners are not expressing any displeasure over what they are seeing and hearing on TV may indicate that they are, actually, getting what they want, or as Mr. Shaw's witticism suggests, that they are merely getting what they deserve.

In any case, we are concerned here, not with the complacent, uncomplaining majority, but with the dissatisfied, rebellious minority.

Let us assume, then, that you care and that you want to know and act. How do you proceed?

Individually, you may write letters to your local station owners, to the networks, to sponsors, even to the advertising agencies that work for sponsors. You will be told that your letters won't count; that no one will pay any attention to them. This is not entirely true. The managers of our mass media may have the "million" mentality. They may think big in dollars and in size of audiences. But they are, after all, individuals like you and me, and the direct approach does have some impact.

The amount of impact, of course, will depend on the tone of your correspondence, its accurate information, and its realistic grasp of broadcasting problems. To achieve such a grasp means that you must watch TV a great deal, you must know how to evaluate what you see, and you must know, not only how to disapprove, but also how to make constructive suggestions.

So-called "crank" letters are not very welcome to broadcasters, and negative, destructive criticism seldom gets any results.

You may act, not only upon the producing side of TV, but also upon the receiving end. You may attempt to persuade children, friends, and neighbors to watch the desirable programs and avoid the undesirable ones. You may urge them to express their own opinions to producers and broadcasters.

In short—you may, if you wish, become a one-man mission for the salvation of television.

The missionary spirit is fine: perhaps all of us should be imbued with more of it, but not all of us, nor even a great many of us, have the inclination or the time to dedicate ourselves unreservedly to the cause of bettering TV. It is wise not to expect too much of ourselves or others, acting as individuals. Write as often as you can, perhaps a bit oftener. Write especially to the deserving programs. Let them know they are being recognized and supported.

Exercise, if you please, your right not to buy a sponsor's product or services. He does not deny you that right. He is extremely sensitive to what he thinks are your desires in this matter. There is nothing like a democratic campaign of disregard and inaction to persade a sponsor to change his mind about the programs he is offering.

As long as you fail to indicate decisively, not merely in terms of opinion, but in terms of cash sales, that you do not care for what the sponsor is doing, he will undoubtedly continue to do it. Your role as a customer in America's market place is your most important role in television's picture.

There is a better way to do all these things, and that is to do them together with others. In our complex, modern society, where the individual must contend constantly with giant, impersonal forces, organization is widely recognized as an expedient road to human progress.

The individual who wants better television may organize to achieve his ends. There is, in fact, an excellent beginning of such organization in this country. It is known as the listener council movement.

A listener council is a federation of all individuals and

groups in a community who are interested in improving radio and television. The first councils were organized, independently of each other, thirteen years ago in Madison, Wisconsin, and San Francisco. They have now grown to state-wide organizations.

Other cities and regions also have listener councils, notably Greater Cleveland and northern and southern California. It is hoped that the movement will soon grow to national proportions. It has the enthusiastic endorsement of the Federal Communications Commission and the support of all expert observers of broadcasting who are thinking about TV's improvement.

Charles A. Siepmann, in his book *Radio, Television, and Society,** lists eight functions of a listener council.

1. To collect and publicize essential facts on the present state of broadcasting.

2. To facilitate and encourage discriminative listening to worthwhile programs.

3. To bring pressure on stations to eliminate abuses.

4. To voice the needs of the community by preparing blueprints of worthwhile programs to be executed by a station.

5. To provide listeners with opportunity to meet and discuss their interests in radio (and TV).

6. By means of bulletins and circulars to alert listeners to important developments in radio (and TV).

7. To carry its members' views to the Federal Communications Commission, whether with reference to matters of policy raised in public hearings before the F.C.C. or to the renewal of a given station's license.

8. To influence not only radio (and TV) but the press by

\* Oxford University Press, 1950.

correspondence and prepared articles on radio (and TV) as a social force.

This is an ambitious program. What are its prospects of success? What are some of its pitfalls?

The first, and most important, "don't" offered by those who have had experience with listener councils is: Don't have representatives of the broadcasting industry as members or as financial supporters. Co-operate with the industry on a friendly basis, but maintain complete independence.

There is a record of attempts by industry to dominate listener councils, and even the chairman of the F.C.C., Mr. Wayne Coy, states flatly that a listener council "must keep free of all entangling alliances. Its integrity as the true, uninfluenced representative of the listener must be above suspicion."

A serious problem faced by all listener councils, as by all volunteer organizations, is the matter of funds. A council in the Midwest, which accepts financial support from local stations, notes in its treasurer's annual report for the year 1949–1950 a total cash expendable figure of $663.08. This is hardly a sufficient sum with which to do battle along the broad fronts outlined by Mr. Siepmann.

To study industry laws and rules, to acquire an understanding of the practical business of broadcasting, to seek the advice of specialists, to make a systematic, continuing study of programming, to publicize and promote—all these tasks require not only unstinting devotion of hours and energies but also money.

Organizations and individuals joining the movement must find means of raising effective funds or see their efforts limited to a sort of noble-minded but peripheral harassment of the television broadcasters, not taken too seriously by the industry.

That such is the regrettable case, at present, must be recognized in an experience, in 1949, of the Southern California Association for Better Radio and Television, one of the three distinguished pioneers of the listener council movement in the United States.

The association made a survey of television programs scheduled between 6 P.M. and 9 P.M. on Los Angeles stations for one week. It found no crime programs on KFI-TV. Here is what it found on the other stations: "91 murders, 7 stage holdups, 3 kidnappings, 10 thefts, 4 burglaries, 2 cases of arson, 2 jailbreaks, 1 murder by explosion of 15 to 20 people, 2 suicides, 1 case of blackmail. Cases of assault and battery—too numerous to tabulate. Also cases of attempted murder. Much of the action takes place in saloons. Brawls too numerous to mention, also drunkenness. Crooked judges, crooked sheriffs, crooked juries."

Mrs. Clara S. Logan, president of the association, asked the Los Angeles stations for the substitution of "acceptable programs which would be suitable for family viewing and listening." The southern California survey received national attention. Editors, educators, even some TV station managers outside California, joined in a chorus urging a cleanup.

What was the result? According to *Time Magazine*, December 19, 1949: "The Los Angeles stations had no comment, except for KNBH, which replied that her [Mrs. Logan's] action would only call attention to the very things she disliked and thereby create further interest in them."

On March 14, 1950, the F.C.C.'s Mr. Coy said: "Last week the association informed me that not one of the stations that carried the crime programs had offered to talk over the survey, not one had indicated that it wanted to correct the situation, although an improvement has been noted in the early evening programs of the NBC station. This is certainly not a very encouraging attitude on the part of the members of an industry that makes so much of its sensitivity to public opinion."

To have achieved an "improvement" on even one station is an accomplishment for which the southern California listener group is to be congratuled, but one must also ask about the duration and scope of the improvement. Generally, on TV, has there been a crescendo or diminuendo in the symphony of horror and crime? Walk, do not run, to your nearest TV set for the answer.

Let us suppose, however, that the listener council movement can overcome the fundamental handicaps of citizen apathy, industry domination, and lack of funds. Let us assume that it has great numbers of members who listen, view, compile facts and figures, publicize, promote—in sum, do all the things the experts urge it to do in the full and proper way. Could it effect a direct improvement in TV?

Mrs. Logan, leader of the southern California group, has said that she and her associates are working along the line that the Federal Communications Commission intends by law to license broadcasting only in the public interest and that an aroused, interested, informed listener group alone can support the F.C.C.

Specifically, an instance testing this course of action would proceed in the following fashion.

TV stations are licensed, at present, for one year. Each year they apply to the F.C.C. in Washington for a renewal of their licenses to operate in the public interest. Assume that a particular TV station had a poor record in the opinion of a local listener group. Assume that when this station applied for the renewal of its license, the F.C.C. had in its docket a full file on this station's past performance, compiled accurately by the listener council. Assume, further, that the F.C.C., contrary to its own past record, took a courageous and forthright stand and refused to renew the station's license.

Two things might conceivably happen. The aggrieved licensee might plead repentance and promise to reform if given another chance. Or, the station's license might be transferred to a new owner who promised to better his predecessor's record. TV stations are deemed excellent investments, and there is no dearth of applicants waiting for an opportunity to secure a license.

In either case, however, the owner granted the license, old or new, would be at a disadvantage in competing with other stations in his area for sponsor revenue. He would, in order to live up to his promise to behave, have to refuse to carry objectionable but profitable network programs, and he would have to "fill in" the time periods vacated with inexpensive local programs which might lose him audiences, or provide expensive local programs, paying for them out of his own pocket.

It is a fact that the best talent in TV tends to gravitate toward the three big centers of network production, New York, Hollywood, and Chicago. To search for and develop new local performers requires talented writers, producers, directors. These latter, usually, find their way to the big three centers of program origination.

Besides, the technical equipment necessary to produce "big time" shows is very costly. In short, a local "fill-in" effort is expensive and the results are doubtful. Our hypothetical, well-meaning local licensee would suffer loss of revenue while his competitors reaped unfair advantage.

To balance the situation would require that all local stations in a given area be compelled to synchronize their "good" behavior. How this could be done, with present differing dates for the renewal of licenses, is a problem few realistic experts would venture to tackle.

Actually, the quandary results from the fact that, while your local licensee is subject, through the F.C.C., to your will, the station owner's real customer—the sponsor—is not. Consequently, when listener groups speak of bringing pressure on licensees, they would be wise to consider carefully the difficulties inherent in the situation, and the possible consequences of their action.

Most assuredly, this is not to be misconstrued as an argument for bringing no pressure at all to bear upon station owners. But zeal ought to be governed by wisdom, and to substitute one unfairness for another is not in the American tradition of fair play. The ethical as well as the mechanical problems of this complicated matter are fundamental. The question is: Are you, a citizen who operates, more or less, on a free-enterprise basis in your own activity, willing to compel a fellow citizen to accept government regulation in his field—an area admittedly serving the public interest, but one over which there is profound and sincere disagreement concerning the nature of the service?

To raise the question is not to say that there is no answer. Undoubtedly an answer exists: it must exist. As suggested in an earlier chapter, the final decision as to what kind of television we shall have rests upon the informed, or uninformed, will of the people, expressed or unexpressed. Ultimately, it may be a matter that only Congress can resolve.

The American Bar Association has a Committee on Motion Pictures, Radio Broadcasting and Comics in Relation to the Administration of Justice. Arthur J. Freund of St. Louis is the chairman. The vice-chairman is the governor of California, Earl Warren; the secretary, the head of the Bureau of Prisons of the Department of Justice, James V. Bennett.

In an address to this committee, in Washington, D. C., November 8, 1948, Mr. Freund spoke about crime portrayals in the mass media. Mr. Freund made it quite clear that his group was opposed to any present restrictive legislation in this field. He made it equally clear, however, that the present industry codes are not operating wholly and effectively in the public interest.

"We are all anxious to prevent legislative intemperance," Mr. Freund said, "and yet we cannot escape the historian's view that what is considered as intemperance in one decade often becomes an accepted and fixed public and governmental policy in another. In 1890, the Sherman Antitrust Act was enacted. . . . There were many of the representatives of industry of that day who fought the antitrust legislation as contrary to the principles of our Constitution and declared that the curbs imposed would be destructive to our way of life.

"The battle was fought in Congress, in the press, and in public debates upon these lines. And yet, with a complete acceptance of the doctrine of free enterprise in our economic system, the legislation was enacted and there is no competent statesman who today would advocate its repeal. . . . A decade and a half later the same battle against restriction upon personal habits was fought when the Pure Food and Drug Act was passed in 1906.

". . . No one who expects to remain in office today would advocate the repeal of the Pure Food and Drug Act. . . . If we do not consider now the steps and methods of learning the actual, vital facts of the problems before us, and, having the facts, deal with the problems intelligently, legislation which you and I would now deem intemperate is, in my considered judgment, inevitable; and neither the great prestige of the American Bar Association nor the powerful resources of the media will be able to prevent it."

Mr. Freund's remarks apply directly to crime programs on TV, but they also furnish an arresting and authoritative insight into the larger problem of the three-way public-industry-government relationship in broadcasting. The reader is invited to judge for himself whether or not the broadcasting industry, at present, is dealing intelligently with the problem of TV programming. In these chapters, care has been exercised to present all pertinent points of view on the case fairly.

If Mr. Freund's prophecy of legislative action is, eventually, to come to pass, then, perhaps, the greatest contribution that listener councils can make lies in the awakening of the public, as a whole, to an aroused interest in the problem, and to an effort to think the matter through to a final making up of its own mind about what sort of programs it wants and how they may be obtained. All available studies disclose that there is little discussion among citizens concerning the character of the broadcasting system they have in this country and the possible alternatives.

Listener councils can spearhead the attack on this ignorance. They can, undoubtedly, stimulate public thinking on the subject, spread abroad the facts, encourage everywhere, in homes, schools, community, organizations, an alert, informed, critical, and continuing campaign of public appraisal of TV. They can keep up the pressure, "broadcast" the conviction, with enthusiasm, that, no matter how difficult the problem may seem at present, it is not insoluble.

This nation, many experts agree, can have a better pattern of broadcasting without sacrificing its traditional method of commercial operation within the framework of public interest. It has been done in other industries. There is no valid reason, say the experts, why it cannot be done in television.

Human resistance to progress is proverbial. But it is the faith and the hope of democracy that this resistance can be dissolved. In the slow but irresistible process of dissolution on the TV front, listener councils can be the great fact-gatherers, the great teachers, the great persuaders.

# 8

## education's challenge in TV

W̶HAT ARE the school officials of the United States—the superintendents, the principals, and the teachers—doing about television?

What can they do?

Some teachers—like some parents—appear to be running away from the TV problem. In May, 1950, as reported in the New York *Times*, a Bergenfield, New Jersey, second-grade teacher announced that at the end of the term she would resign and go to Nevada where there were, as yet, no television sets or stations. She could no longer stand the daily struggle to teach the three R's to little Lone Rangers.

"Why, of the 20 children in my class, 19 have television sets at home," she told a "slightly amazed" Bergenfield Board of Education. "The parents seem to welcome it as an easy way of keeping their children entertained. It's no wonder they are bored by school. How can I compete with Hopalong Cassidy? I have the feeling my pupils expect me to go into a song-and-dance act."

The teacher expected to find peace in Reno, where she

intended to continue her professional work. She hoped
that TV would have outgrown its "silliness" by the time
it reached Nevada. Television, properly controlled, she
thought, could be of use at home and at school. The Bergenfield teacher said that, from 1946 to 1949, she had taught
school in Nevada, where little boys play cowboy, too—but
"realistically," not like Captain Video.

Of course, if TV has not outgrown its "silliness" by the
time the coaxial cable leaps the Sierra Nevadas, the ex-
Bergenfield schoolma'am may have to face her problem all
over again. Non-TV havens can be expected to diminish
steadily within United States territorial limits. That is probably why an increasing number of teachers already are
realizing that an important part of their job is to help TV
outgrow its silliness, to use it properly so that it can become
of use at home and at school.

While few of the nation's teachers are actually withdraw-
ing under fire, there is evidence that many teachers still are
mentally resisting television, shutting it out of both their
personal and professional considerations. Small spot samplings, personal interviews with teachers, principals, and
school superintendents have disclosed this attitude to be
fairly common.

A Massachusetts poll of grade-school teachers asked: "Do
you discuss TV critically and constructively with your students?" and "Do you personally view TV at home?" Many
answered "yes" to both questions, but a considerable number replied in this fashion: "No. Personally I do not enjoy
television. Would rather read a good book." "Occasionally."
"I cannot afford a set." "Sometimes at a friend's home."

The Massachusetts sample clearly suggests that many
teachers are not "up" on TV. Their pupils are excited and

interested in programs and the teachers have no way of constructively exploiting this excitement and interest because they don't know what the children are talking about. Some teacher resistance may be attributable to a prejudice against all audio-video aids—a prejudice based on the teacher's fear that she will lose prestige, authority, and perhaps eventually even her job.

One hesitates to suggest that all teachers ought immediately to go out and buy themselves TV sets. But when youngsters who spend more hours a week watching television than they spend in school are taught by teachers who are largely without television sets, it may follow that the teachers are not fully availing themselves of what could be an important educational tool.

Perhaps the gap can be closed somewhat by having TV sets in the schools, but this is not the complete answer. While our children live in one world before and after school hours, and our teachers in another, the classroom becomes a kind of no man's land instead of a meeting ground for teacher and student.

Fortunately, many imaginative teachers are not waiting for others to close the gap between the child's TV world and his classroom world. Miss Barbara Alice Wolfe, a teacher in White Plains, New York, writing in the January, 1950, issue of the *Journal of the Association for Education by Radio*, offers a fine approach.

"Preferring to turn the enemy's guns to our advantage, we decide to make clear to our students the relationship between the delights of TV and the rewards of study. . . . Why let my students think of scientific marvels in terms of Superman and Buck Rogers when I can introduce them to Jules Verne, H. G. Wells, and Sir Francis Bacon. . . .

One can absorb strength and beauty from every element of life, if only the proper associations be made, consciously or otherwise. Guidance quickens the process and guidance is our job.

". . . Let's make TV a contributing force to the betterment of our work—let's make television a topic of conversation in as well as outside of school, and while we're waiting for sets, promised programs, and more time for elaborate procedures, let's bring TV into class discussion in other ways—by casual reference or interpolated remarks. . . .

"Don't let's depend on someone else for video material of educational value, let's you and I and all of us together make everything on and about video educationally valuable to ourselves and our TV-wise charges!"

Many observers are urging that schools include courses in their curricula which teach the critical evaluation of TV, and of other mass media. These observers argue that we are leaving the age of the spoken and written word and entering the era of pictures.

It is high time, they say, that our classrooms caught up with the outside world. We teach our children standards in grammar and literature: why not also teach them how to look at television, read the funnies, go to the movies? Our colleges do, in some cases, give courses in the evaluation of the media, but these are mainly for students interested in professional careers.

It should be the other way around, declare the contenders for this theory: the inculcation of critical capacities should not wait upon higher education: it should begin in the lowest grades where, certainly, the contact between children and the mass media is the sharpest.

All of the foregoing are suggestions for strengthening, in

the school, the child's discriminative ability at the receiving end of TV. Are the educators doing anything to improve the flow of television's material at its source—the production end?

The overwhelming majority of school systems in this country (for this is admittedly a task most individual schools, even colleges, cannot tackle alone) are doing nothing. They are leaving the matter entirely in the hands of the commercial broadcasters in the hope that some forces, somehow, will bring about an elevation of TV's cultural standards. However, all candid observers—in the industry, in government, and in education—agree that this is a forlorn hope in the foreseeable future.

Some school systems, notably in Philadelphia, Baltimore, and in Chicago, are co-operating on the production end with local TV stations. The stations provide time and facilities, and the schools themselves produce or assist in the production of programs which are telecast during classroom hours. The schools, in many possible ways, arrange for TV sets in classrooms and auditoriums.

This co-operation has its merits and limitations. The merits are that the schools are making a valiant effort to introduce some responsible thinking into TV programming. The limitations are that funds available for program production are inadequate, and that the educators are generally untrained in the highly specialized skills of program production. Added complications are the difficulty of synchronizing program hours with classroom schedules, the problem of obtaining suitable viewing conditions, and the lack of teachers who know how to use program material before and after telecasts.

It is a fine thing to have a regular schedule of programs

coming into the schools during study hours. But it is well to ask what the results will be when students, accustomed to the more vigorous fare of commercial TV, are often plainly bored by school broadcasts.

Another hazard in the co-operation between schools and local stations is the problem of what happens to the school program when the station sells its daytime periods? At present, the broadcasters do not yet have their maximum daytime TV audiences. If and when they do, the past record of school-station relationships in radio indicates that the schools will lose their present time allotments to commercial sponsors.

Some educators are considering the idea of accepting sponsorship for in-school programs, but this is a dangerous path to tread. Many observers question whether even a strongly regulated alliance between schools and advertisers is at all advisable.

The experts agree that the schools should continue, as long as they are permitted, to co-operate vigorously with the commercial station owners. The experience gained cannot but help immeasurably to clarify educational TV goals and to train personnel.

A critically friendly eye cast by schools on local stations, and a disposition to help publicize good commercial programs as well as to express dissatisfaction with bad ones, are both important phases of the school's long-range relationship with broadcasters, parent-teacher associations, and organized listener groups.

It would be wise, however, for school systems not to place too much emphasis in their plans on co-operation with commercial broadcasters. Commercial and educational aims are not identical.

A few educators propose seriously to sidetrack TV alto-gether as far as the schools are concerned and to put what-ever funds are available into educational films prepared ex-pressly for classroom use. The anti-TV educators argue that films are cheaper than television, are superior in quality, and can be used as often as each teacher's needs require. While this point of view is not without merit, interest in TV is likely to grow among the majority of educators, who are concerned with audio-visual aids.

The really important area toward which educators are moving in TV is one marked "Education's Ownership and Operation of Its Own Stations." In this effort, the educators are fortunate in having the strong support of Miss Frieda Hennock, of the Federal Communications Commission. Miss Hennock has said that she "can think of no group more fit to lend direction to broadcasting in this country than our educational organizations."

Most educators are undoubtedly eager, in theory, to "lend direction"—but a crisis impends in educational broadcasting in which they must practically prove their enthusiasm. Here are the facts.

In September, 1948, the Federal Communications Com-mission "froze" the processing of applications for the con-struction of new television stations in order, first, to resolve certain complicated technical problems. It is expected that this "freeze" will be lifted sometime in 1951. The commis-sioners will then face at least several hundred applications already on file, with more coming in constantly. There is only a limited amount of space on broadcasting's street for TV stations. The air cannot accommodate, in an orderly fashion, an infinite number.

In the Spring of 1950, the chairman of the F.C.C.,

Wayne Coy, said that by 1953 he expected to see 600 to 800 TV stations on the air. That figure will, no doubt, be cut considerably, due to the anticipated scarcity of construction materials arising out of the national emergency, and to the retarded growth of the TV audience, resulting from the cutback in the manufacture of television receivers—a smaller audience inspiring fewer stations.

Nevertheless, with anticipated earnings expected to be large, there will still, undoubtedly, be more requests for commercial licenses than there are channels available. The competition for these available channels will be, to say the least, severe.

Of the 107 TV stations on the air early in 1951, only one, WOI, at Ames, Iowa, was owned by an educational institution—the Iowa State College of Agriculture and Mechanic Arts. Of the more than 350 applications for licenses pending at the beginning of the year, only a small number had been submitted by schools, colleges, or municipalities.

The basic reason for this poor representation of educational institutions in TV is lack of the money required to construct and operate so expensive an instrument of communication as a television station. Our schools and the educational agencies of our government struggle traditionally against the handicap of low budgets. Theoretically we accord high honor in our way of life to education and culture in the United States, but actually workers in the realm of the mind figuratively go begging for crusts of bread.

This poverty of status for education in our society casts a ragged cloak over all aspects of educational broadcasting. It accounts partly for the ineffective showing that the schools have made in radio, both AM and FM. Twice in the history of broadcasting in this country, our educators have had opportunities to grasp and exploit intensively the air potential—and twice they have failed to do so.

If educational stations are not equipped to compete successfully for public attention with the commercial broadcasters, they can have no prestige in the community. If they have no prestige, they cannot attract professional writers, producers, directors, or artists. They cannot even excite the interest of most of the faculty on the campus, who are often reluctant to take part in the broadcast work of their own schools.

The estimated cost of a single educational television station covering one state is between three and five million dollars. New school buildings and new facilities for instruction are everywhere desperately needed for the growing armies of children clamoring to be taught. Teachers are rightly demanding and only now beginning to receive anything like just pay for their important work. In the face of such financial pressures, what school board is likely to decide that educational television must have priority over all other serious considerations requiring budgetary support?

And yet, the educators must realize that television represents their most spectacular opportunity on the American broadcasting scene. As these pages are given into the hands of the printer (January 1951) there is a strong possibility that the F.C.C. may set aside, for the exclusive use of the educational broadcasters, a portion of the television channels that are still to be distributed.

The commission is holding hearings in Washington, D. C., on the matter of educational television. A Joint Committee of Educational Broadcasters has made an impressive case for a set-aside, and there are signs that the F.C.C. is favorably disposed, in principle, to the committee's petition for a reservation of channels.

If, for any reasons, the Federal Communications Commission should decide not to reserve television channels for the exclusive use of educational broadcasters, then, of course, education's last ship will have sailed past the television horizon. Educational broadcasters will not be able to compete, financially, on equal terms with the commercial broadcasters, and, most likely, education will be doomed to make the same poor showing in TV that it made in radio— if not a poorer one.

On the other hand, should the F.C.C. make the set-aside, the battle will have been only half-won. The educators must then, somehow, find ways and means of raising the large sums of money which are necessary to put them significantly in the TV picture.

They must file their applications for TV licenses with the F.C.C.; they must battle for them fervently in commission hearings in their own localities; and they must actually build, operate, and maintain their stations efficiently, imaginatively, and constructively; otherwise they may lose their exclusive, noncompetitive status.

Television channels in the United States will always be far too much in demand by legitimate business interests to be wasted or ineffectually used by educators; and what the F.C.C. may grant, it may also take away.

All parents and citizens who are concerned with their children's growth in a world of mass media which for its part is concerned primarily with business considerations have a right to know these facts and understand their stake in them.

They must be willing, as taxpayers, to bear the financial burdens involved. They must bring their deep interest in this serious matter to the notice of their school boards and their representatives in state, city, and national government.

It is highly improbable, for reasons that we have examined, that anything will be done in the foreseeable future to lift the standards of television programs at their source if the great majority of TV stations that will be built and operated in the United States come into the hands of the commercial broadcasters.

The home's only defense against TV's negative influence will be the strengthening of children's powers to discriminate and view programs selectively. The people will have lost, finally, their right to complain.

On the other hand, the prospect would be encouraging if there are a sufficient number of TV stations owned by educational institutions and truly operated "in the public interest, convenience, and necessity," if the educators have the money with which to attract and hold competent writing and production talent and properly to promote their programs so that the public may know about them and be persuaded to listen.

Educational broadcasting may then be able to show our children, and all the people, something new and better in TV.

The educational broadcasters will be able to test once and for all the distasteful proposition that American TV, at present, reflects United States tastes. Committed primarily to the movement of ideas rather than of merchandise, education's TV can, perhaps, slowly lift the general cultural level in this nation, and persuade the commercial broadcasters to raise their own sights.

Many observers are convinced that such a prospect is a noble but impractical dream.

The American people can—if they will—make it television's awakening.